ABOUT
HOW THINGS WORK

PUBLISHER	Joseph R. DeVarennes
PUBLICATION DIRECTOR	Kenneth H. Pearson
ADVISORS	Roger Aubin
	Robert Furlonger
EDITORIAL SUPERVISOR	Jocelyn Smyth
PRODUCTION MANAGER	Ernest Homewood
PRODUCTION ASSISTANTS	Martine Gingras Kathy Kishimoto
	Catherine Gordon Peter Thomlison
CONTRIBUTORS	Alison Dickie Nancy Prasad
	Bill Ivy Lois Rock
	Jacqueline Kendel Merebeth Switzer
	Anne Langdon Dave Taylor
	Sheila Macdonald Alison Tharen
	Susan Marshall Donna Thomson
	Pamela Martin Pam Young
	Colin McCance
SENIOR EDITOR	Robin Rivers
EDITORS	Brian Cross Ann Martin
	Anne Louise Mahoney Mayta Tannenbaum
PUBLICATION ADMINISTRATOR	Anna Good
ART AND DESIGN	Richard Comely Ronald Migliore
	Robert B. Curry Penelope Moir
	George Elliott Marion Stuck
	Marilyn James Bill Suddick
	Robert Johanssen Sue Wilkinson

Canadian Cataloguing in Publication Data

Main entry under title:

Questions kids ask about how things work

(Questions kids ask; 22)
ISBN 0-7172-2561-5

1. Technology—Miscellanea—Juvenile literature.
2. Science—Miscellanea—Juvenile literature.
2. Children's questions and answers.
I. Smyth, Jocelyn.   II. Comely, Richard.   III. Series.

T48.Q47 1988   j600   C89-093171-2

Questions Kids Ask . . . about HOW THINGS WORK

continued

How does a vending machine know that you've put the right money in?

The coins you put in a vending machine have to pass a tricky obstacle course before the machine will give you anything. The coin first passes a series of slots. Small coins will fall through a small slot, while larger coins run on to a larger slot. When coins go through a slot, they fall toward a trap door. The trap door will only open if the coin is the right weight for its size. After the coin goes through the trap door, it passes a special magnet. The magnet will catch any fake coins that people might try to use instead of real money. If the coin passes the magnet test, it keeps falling. Finally it pushes open the last door. A special release mechanism then lets you have whatever you've selected from the machine! If a coin gets stuck at any time, push the "reject" lever. This will push the coin into the escape chute to be returned to you—if you're lucky!

How does sound get from a radio station to your radio?

When you speak, the sound travels through the air in waves like ripples in a pond do. But a radio announcer could never speak loudly enough to talk to people across the country by using sound waves, and anyway some people might not want to listen.

In a radio station, the speaker talks into a microphone. This turns the sounds into an electric current.

The current is then turned into special radio waves. They are sent to an antenna that transmits them long distances. These waves travel much faster than sound—and they travel silently.

In your radio, a much smaller antenna picks up the radio waves. Other parts of your radio turn them back into sound that you can hear.

DID YOU KNOW . . . radio waves travel at the speed of light (300 000 kilometres per second or 186 000 miles per second).

What is a compact disc?

Have you ever seen a compact disc? It is silvery and reflects many different colors. When you put it in a compact disc player, you hear the sounds that have been recorded on it.

To make a compact disc, people first record music or voices onto a digital tape. Then the tape is run through a laser machine. The laser reacts to the sounds and cuts pits of different sizes in a master disc. These pits are like a secret code. The compact disc player has another laser inside it that can "read" the secret code on the disc and turn it back into sound.

Plastic copies are made of the master disc. Each one is coated in aluminum, which makes it shine, and covered with clear plastic. Now it's ready to play in your CD player.

What does an antenna do?

Antennas are used to send and receive radio, television and radar signals. Transmitting antennas send radio waves from high towers to the radio transmitter. Receiving antennas receive radio waves. The antenna is pointed in the direction of the broadcasting station for the best reception possible.

Television antennas must be placed very high above the ground in order to pick up signals.

A radar antenna sends radio waves in the form of a beam, then it collects the echoes of these waves when they return.

Antennas come in all shapes and sizes. Some are tall towers, others are huge dishes. The one in your radio may be just a centimetre (1/3 of an inch) long!

How can a calculator always get the right answer?

How do you add two and three on your fingers? Hold up two fingers on one hand and three on the other. Now count up. One, two, three, four, five. Right! But try adding 27 and 42—you'll run out of fingers.

Imagine that every time you press a number on a calculator, it holds up just the right number of electronic "fingers." When you tell it to add, it gets ready to count. Then, when you put in the next number, it holds up that number of electronic fingers on another hand. Finally it does the counting and displays the answer.

Because the calculator is a machine, it always counts each number in exactly the same way. It also works very fast, so it gives the result almost immediately. It can subtract, multiply, divide and do many other calculations as well.

How does a photocopier work?

Have you ever put a paper doily on top of a cake and dusted icing sugar over it? If you have, you know that the fine powdered sugar falls through the holes in the doily and leaves the pattern of the lace on the cake.

A photocopier works in a similar way. A flash of light shines the pattern that is on your paper through to a cylinder inside the machine. Electricity makes black powder stick to the cylinder in the exact places where there is black on your piece of paper. A fresh piece of paper rolls over the cylinder, and the black powder is transferred from the cylinder to the blank paper. The paper is then heated so the powder is absorbed into it.

Presto! Your copy is ready.

Do computers have memories?

Where do you store your belongings at school? Perhaps you have a cubby hole or a locker. A computer has many thousands of electronic cubby holes inside it. When you enter information into a computer, it stores one piece of information in each cubby hole.

In time, of course, these cubby holes will get filled up. To avoid this problem, many computers can send extra information into overflow storage, such as a floppy disk. It's rather like you putting extra things from your locker into a bag and taking them home until you really need them.

Why does a key open a lock?

Have you ever seen a baby playing with a shape sorter? The baby has to match each of the shapes with the openings in the toy. A square shape will not go through a triangle-shaped hole in the toy.

A key for a simple type of lock works in the same way. The special shape on the end of the key matches an opening inside the lock.

As you push the key into the lock, the notches like a saw in the key lift up a series of vertical pins that block the way. When the key has lifted all the pins, the key turns the bolt mechanism and releases the lock.

If you use the wrong key, it simply won't turn.

DID YOU KNOW . . . a similar lock-and-key system was developed in ancient Egypt almost 4000 years ago!

How does a compass work?

To understand how a compass works you first have to know something about the special properties of the earth. The earth is surrounded by a magnetic field. It's as if an enormous bar magnet is running through the core of the earth with one end near the North Pole and the other end close to the South Pole.

A compass is an instrument for determining direction. The simplest compass has a small magnetic bar, or needle, which rests on a pin so it can spin around. All directions, including north, south, west and east, are marked on the compass. The north tip of the bar is pointed or colored so you can distinguish it easily. Because the bar is magnetic, it lines itself up with the magnetic forces in the earth. The north tip points to the magnetic north near the North Pole and the other end points south.

So if you want to head north, go in the direction the colored tip indicates. If you want to travel south, head in the opposite direction.

How does a kaleidoscope work?

Look through the peephole of a kaleidoscope—you may be amazed at the number of colored patterns you can see. Someone watching your kaleidoscope from the other end will just see bits of colored plastic falling in a heap.

If you look carefully at the patterns you see through the peephole, you will see that each one is made up of identical segments.

Inside a kaleidoscope are many carefully arranged mirrors. One mirror reflects all the colored plastic pieces onto another mirror. This mirror reflects them onto another mirror—and when you see the same untidy heap of bits reflected several times, it looks like a beautiful pattern.

How does a camera work?

A camera is a box which has a tiny hole in it that can let light shine in. When you take a picture, the shutter, which normally blocks the hole, opens for a split second. Light shines through a glass lens into the camera. The lens allows the light rays to bend. They leave the image, or picture, of what you've just photographed on the film, which is sensitive to light.

To develop the film, photographers use special chemicals which make the film turn the same color as the light that shone on it.

DID YOU KNOW. . . if the object you are photographing moves while the shutter is open, the image on the film will be blurred.

How do motion pictures move?

Whenever you see something with your eyes, your brain goes on seeing it for one-tenth of a second *after* your eyes stop seeing it. Movies "move" because of this fact. Moving pictures consist of a series of still photographs called frames that are taken very quickly, one after the other. They are then played back at the same speed. For example, a movie camera might take hundreds of pictures of you picking up a cup. In each one, the cup would be just a tiny bit nearer your mouth. If you were shown these pictures at the rate of more than ten per second, your brain would still have the last picture in mind when it saw the next one. The pictures blur together to give the impression of smooth motion.

DID YOU KNOW . . . most home movies show about 16 frames per second. Better quality movies often have 24 frames per second. If you see a very old movie, you will notice that the action is jerky because there are fewer frames per second.

13

How do planes fly?

Planes can fly because of their wings. They don't flap them up and down like birds, but they do use their wings to get into the air. To understand how, it helps to look at their shape.

The bottom surface of a wing is flat, while the top is curved. This means that the surface of the top is longer than the surface of the bottom. As the plane moves forward, air flowing over the top surface has a longer way to go, so it must travel faster in order to keep up with the rest of the air—that is, its speed is greater. When the speed is greater, the pressure is less. In other words, air pressure on top of the wing is less than the air pressure on the bottom. Because the pressure is greater on the bottom, the wings are pushed upward, and they carry the rest of the plane up with them. This upward force caused by air passing over the wings is called "lift."

How does an airplane move forward?

There are two main types of airplanes: propeller airplanes and jet airplanes. When a propeller whizzes around, it pushes air behind it in a broad stream. When a jet engine is on, it sends out a thin stream of very hot air and gas. The backward rush of air causes a reaction—the airplane moves forward.

You can see how the backward rush of air causes something to move forward by blowing up a balloon and letting the air escape. The balloon will shoot forward away from the stream of escaping air.

What keeps a train on the tracks?

Over four hundred years ago in Europe, early railroads were built in the underground mines. Two wooden rails were laid on the ground. Men or horses pulled wagons along the rails. The wagons were full of coal or iron. The wheels had "flanged" wheels. This means that they had a rim on the inner edge that fit over the rail and prevented the wheels from sliding off the rails.

Diesel, electric and steam locomotives have now replaced manpower and horsepower. Steel freight cars and comfortable passenger cars have taken the place of wagons. The powerful locomotives pull these cars along steel tracks instead of wood, but the method of keeping the train on the track is still the same. Flanged metal wheels guide the train along the track. The track consists of two parallel rails attached to wooden ties. The ties are anchored in ballast, consisting of gravel or crushed rock. The rails rest on steel tieplates which hold the rails in place. Spikes fasten the rails and tieplates to the ties.

So it doesn't matter if a train is traveling through the mountains, down a long tunnel or around a sharp corner, the train never leaves the tracks—or hardly ever.

DID YOU KNOW . . . there are 1 240 000 kilometres (775 000 miles) of railroads in the word— more than three times the distance to the moon and back.

Why don't you fall out of a roller coaster when it turns upside down?

Hand in your ticket, climb into your seat, and fasten your safety belt. Slowly the roller coaster starts to move. It pulls lazily up a steep hill, and just as you think it's about to stop . . . whoosh! you plunge down a hill! It turns upside down as it goes around one loop after another.

You might have been too scared to notice, but when you were upside down, your body didn't even push against your shoulder safety strap. That's because an object that is moving in a circle tends to move away from the center of the circle. As you looped the loop, your car—and you—were flung away from the center against its outer edge, the track.

If you want to test this force, called centrifugal force, swing a bucket of water in a windmill fashion around you. If your arm moves quickly enough, the water will stay in the bucket even when it is upside down.

DID YOU KNOW . . . if the roller coaster were going slowly around a loop the loop and you weren't wearing a seatbelt, you *would* fall out!

16

How does a magician saw a person in half?

"And for my next trick," says the magician, "I will place my assistant into this box, and saw the box in two!"

A smiling assistant climbs into the box. "Your head comes out here," says the magician, "and your hands here." The assistant's head and hands appear through small holes. "And there are holes for your feet here." Out come two feet.

A saw is produced. The blade slices wickedly through the box. Metal sheets are inserted at the cut ends so we don't see the sliced body as the magician turns the two cut sides to the audience. A murmur of amazement runs through the audience. Yet the assistant is still smiling.

The box is put back into the first position. Out come the metal dividers. Abracadabra! The assistant is released, unharmed and still smiling.

How does the magician do it? *There is another person hidden in the lower half of the box. It is this person's feet that you see sticking out. The assistant you see curls up tight in the top half of the box!*

17

How do lighthouses work?

Imagine being the captain of a ship and trying to sail along the coast on a dark, foggy night. Then you see a familiar flash from a lighthouse. Thank goodness! Now you know which way to steer.

A lighthouse is a tall, narrow building with a very powerful light on its roof. On a clear night, some can be seen from a distance of 40 kilometres (25 miles). The light rotates so that it can be seen by ships in all directions. The spinning of the light makes it appear to flash on and off. The speed of the flashes can be altered and used in a sequence or code to warn sailors of special dangers.

Some lighthouses send sound signals as well. When it is very foggy, a loud siren, horn or cannon can be used as a warning. Lighthouses also send radio and radar signals. Ships can read these signals with special equipment and judge their position.

Years ago, lighthouse keepers lived inside lighthouses and operated the lights. Today, many lighthouses are run by machines.

How does a lightbulb work?

Most of us take for granted that we can simply flick a switch and a lightbulb will light up a room. But what makes the lightbulb work?

A lightbulb is made up of three parts: a bulb, a base and a filament. The filament is a coil of thin wire. When you turn on a light switch, electricity flows through the filament. The filament is made to resist the flow of electricity. This causes the filament to heat up to almost 2500°C (4500°F), which is so hot that it glows and gives off light. The kind of lightbulbs found in most homes are *incandescent,* which means "glowing with heat."

The bulb around the filament keeps air away from it so that the filament doesn't burn up. Most bulbs contain a mixture of gases which help the filament last longer. When a lightbulb burns out, it is usually because the filament is broken or has evaporated.

The base of a lightbulb is usually shaped to screw into a socket, which connects it to the electrical outlet.

What is neon?

The air around you is made up of different gases, such as oxygen and carbon dioxide.

Another type of gas, called neon, is found in tiny quantities in the air. You have probably seen neon lights or signs. They are glowing tubes of light that are shaped into words or pictures.

Neon lights are produced by removing the air from a glass tube and filling it with neon gas. An electric current is sent from one end of the tube to the other. Energy is released and the neon glows orange-red. If mercury is added, the neon glows blue-green.

DID YOU KNOW. . . neon light can penetrate fog.

How far can you see with a telescope?

Light from objects far away in space can travel in a straight line to our earth as long as nothing else gets in the way. As a result, telescopes that look into space can help people find objects millions and millions of kilometres (or miles) away.

DID YOU KNOW . . . people who study the sky have to wait for the light from stars to reach their telescopes. Some stars are so far away that it takes years for their light to reach the earth.

Why can't you see across the ocean with a telescope?

A telescope helps you see any object whose light has reached the glass inside it. When you are studying objects on the earth's surface, the farthest you can possibly see is the point where the round earth curves away from you. Light from objects beyond this point cannot travel around the bend.

If you look into the far distance with a telescope, you may see objects coming over the curve in the earth just as you might see a person appearing over the top of a hill. For example, you would see first the head, then the shoulders, and gradually more and more of the body until the whole person was in view. If you look for tall ships at sea through a telescope, you will see first the tip of the mast, then more and more of the mast until the whole ship appears!

What is the difference between a microscope and a telescope?

A microscope and a telescope work in the same way. Both contain curved lenses similar to the one in a magnifying glass. These lenses are arranged so that a small or distant object appears larger.

A telescope is used to study objects that look small because they are far away. A microscope is used to study objects that look small because they really are!

How does water get to the top of a shower?

Imagine that you had a bucket of water and a hose. You could put one end of the hose in the bucket of water and the other end over the shower rod so that it pointed into the bathtub. You could close your eyes, sing your favorite shower song—but no water would come out of the hose. Why not? Water doesn't flow upward.

So how does a shower work?

Somewhere in the area, there is a tank of water that is higher than the top of your shower. It might be up a hill or at the top of a huge, mushroom-shaped water tower. The pressure of water that is up high pushes water along the pipes to your home—and keeps on pushing. Water pressure makes the water go up the pipe to the top of your shower.

When you turn on the taps, a powerful stream of water comes out of the shower nozzle. That's water pressure at work!

How does a toilet know when to stop flushing?

Have you ever looked in the toilet tank? It is about three quarters full of water. Floating on top is a ball attached to a stick. The stick blocks the opening of a water pipe.

If you press the lever to flush the toilet, the water in the tank will empty into the toilet bowl. As the water level in the tank goes down, the ball-shaped object will drop slightly. Then the stick moves, so that water from the pipe can rush into the tank.

Once you stop pressing the lever, no more water can get out into the bowl, so the water level in the tank rises. Up floats the ball on the stick, until the stick blocks the water pipe and no more water can get in.

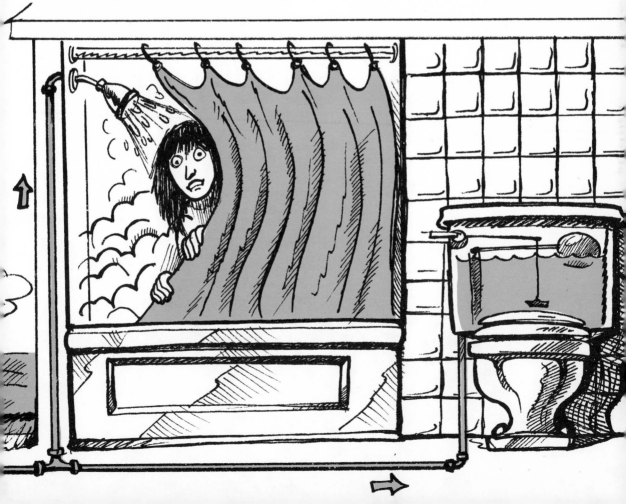

How does toothpaste get in the tube?

If you have ever squeezed too much toothpaste out of the tube, you know that it is impossible to force any back in through the little nozzle. How do people fill toothpaste tubes in the first place?

When they make the tubes, they leave the wide bottom end open. Then they put the caps on the narrow opening at the top. The toothpaste is squeezed in through the bottom end of the tube, which is then sealed up.

This method is used to fill tubes with any squeezable product from shampoo to hand cream.

How does an aerosol can work?

When you shake an aerosol can, you can hear something inside. You might think it's just the insect repellant or whatever, but it's more than that.

The product in the can is mixed with something else: a special gas that is packed down so hard it has turned to liquid. When you push the button on the can, you open a little hole that lets some of the squashed gas out to find more space. As the gas escapes, it carries some of the product with it.

Outside the can, the liquid gas has enough space to expand and turn back to a vapor right away. It leaves thousands of tiny droplets of the product hanging in the air.

DID YOU KNOW . . . the word aerosol really means a cloud of tiny particles hanging in the air. Fog is a natural aerosol.

How does soap get things clean?

Some types of dirt float away easily in water, but other types— particularly greasy things like the fat from French fries—do not.

Soap helps clean away grease because it is made up of tiny bits that have a "head" and "tail." The heads like water, but the tails hate it. In order to escape from it, they bury themselves into the greasy dirt. As more and more of them do so, they pull the grease away in tiny balls that float away in the water.

How do air conditioners work?

Think of the water in a kettle. It starts out as a liquid, but when you heat it, it turns to steam. If you let the water boil for a few minutes, some of this gas will cool on the windows and other surfaces and run down as drops of cold water.

Inside an air conditioner is a special type of liquid called Freon. It travels in circles, turning from liquid to gas and back again, just like water in a kettle. It is piped into a building in liquid form. Air from the building is blown over the pipe and the Freon absorbs most of the heat from the air. A fan blows the cool air back into the building.

The hot Freon gas is taken just outside the building and is squeezed so tightly that it has to turn back into a liquid. As it does so, it lets go of its heat.

The cold Freon liquid is sent back into the building and the cycle begins again.

How do people make sliced bread?

If you tried to slice a loaf of bread, you would probably find it very hard to make each slice the same size. To slice bread, people use a special machine that slices the whole loaf at once. It has a very sharp blade for every slice. The blades can be set to cut thick or thin slices, and the loaf is done in seconds.

The bread slicing machine was the best thing *before* sliced bread!

How does a toaster know when the bread is brown enough?

Look at your toaster. It probably has a little dial that allows you to choose light, medium or dark toast. How does it know one from the other? And why doesn't it break down if you put in dark rye bread?

The secret is behind the dial where a mechanism measures how hot the toaster gets. Toaster manufacturers test how long it takes until a slice of bread is lightly done, medium and well done. Then, instead of labeling the dial with various temperatures, they simply show roughly how dark the toast will be when you set the dial at a certain position. When the toaster reaches the heat that corresponds to the dial setting you have chosen, it turns itself off—whether your toast is light, medium, dark, or totally burned!

How many people can a ferris wheel carry?

Of course, it depends on the size of the ferris wheel. The first one, invented by American engineer G.W. Ferris, was 76 metres (250 feet) high and could carry more than 2000 people! It was built for the World's Columbian Exposition in Chicago in 1893.

Today's ferris wheel is much smaller than the original. A medium-sized ferris wheel is 12 to 14 metres (40 to 45 feet) high, and holds 32 people.

How does an eraser remove pencil marks?

Have you ever used sandpaper on wood? If you have, you know that the scratchy sand is sharp enough to cut off the tiny splinters that make wood feel rough.

An eraser works the same way on pencil marks. The eraser is just hard enough to knock the black substance left by the pencil, called graphite, right off the paper.

Don't rub too hard! If you do, your eraser will start knocking away bits of the paper along with the graphite. You might make a hole in the page.

DID YOU KNOW . . . the highest ferris wheel operating today is ''The Giant Peter'' in Japan. It is 85 metres (278 feet) high and can hold 384 people.

How can you read invisible ink?

Invisible ink is any type of liquid that will not show up on paper. It is only useful if you can make the ink show up when you want to read the message.

One very simple type of invisible ink is milk. If you dip your finger in milk and then write with your moist fingertip on paper, you can write invisible letters. Before you can read the message, the paper must be heated. The milk will turn brown before the paper burns, revealing the secret message.

Another method is to use special pens. One pen contains invisible ink. The second pen contains a chemical which makes the ink visible.

How does a battery work?

Batteries are a part of our everyday life. We use them to run flashlights, portable radios and many of our favorite toys. How do these small metal cylinders work?

A dry cell, which is the most widely used battery, has three main parts: the case which surrounds the battery, called an anode, a rod running through the center, called a cathode, and a fluid that fills up the space between the anode and the cathode. This fluid contains chemicals that react with the anode. The chemical reaction goes on all the time inside a battery, and it produces countless tiny particles called electrons. The electrons are attracted to the cathode, but most move outside of the battery to get there. When a wire loop connects the anode to the cathode, the electrons quickly race through the wire to the cathode and react with chemicals there. The moving electrons produce electricity.

When you place a battery into a flashlight and switch it on, you produce a connection that allows the electrons to move from the anode to the cathode. The moving electrons make the electricity necessary to power your light.

Can you guess why batteries wear out? When all the chemicals in the cathode are used up, the electrons won't race through the wire any more. Without racing electrons, the battery cannot produce electricity.

What is a pacemaker?

Your heart beats steadily all through your life. When you listen to your heartbeat through a doctor's stethescope, you hear a regular double beat: bobom, bobom, bobom.

Sometimes the heart doesn't work properly. For example, it might not beat regularly. A heart that no longer beats regularly may stop beating altogether. To fix this problem, someone invented a tiny machine called a pacemaker. It runs on small batteries. A pacemaker is placed in a person's body by a skilled surgeon. The machine sends the heart little electric shocks to prompt it to beat. Many people have pacemakers. Once they have one, they can live without worrying that their heart may stop.

What are microwaves?

Microwaves are like very short radio waves—they are invisible ripples less than 30 centimetres (a foot) long that can pass through air and even some solids.

When microwaves are switched on in a microwave oven, they make the molecules in the food vibrate. As the molecules vibrate, they rub against each other, creating heat. That's how a microwave oven heats up food.

DID YOU KNOW . . .
microwaves cannot go through metal.

Index _____